Little Santos

"Against all Odds"

Santos Vallejo

Little Santos was short and small, in 3rd grade.

Other kids would make fun of him because he was not tall. This is how he was made.

"Everyone's different, no two are the same." His mother would always tell him, "Don't complain." Just be you and you'll be fine.

Little Santos was labeled with a learning disability. He couldn't read at age 9, but he persisted and wouldn't stop trying. He asked for help time and time again.

"I don't know much about reading," his mother said. She felt helpless and ashamed.

Little Santos cried in prayer, "Dear God please help me now. Give me the brain that Timmy has so I can read books the same as he. I don't want to have a learning disability. I just want to be normal. Is there such a possibility?"

Slowly but surely little Santos grew taller, faster and faster each year.

He met some friendly God sent teachers that helped him overcome his fears.

Graduation finally arrived and little Santos was excited. What would he do? What would he become? He was delighted at all the possibilities.

Little Santos' dreams were crushed. He was told he could only work as a janitor because he had a learning disability.

He refused to believe what he was told and kept praying to God. "God, are there other possibilities?"

Just then, as uncertain as everything in his life, little Santos took a chance. He decided he wanted to be a firefighter. Although, he felt as small as an ant standing next to everyone else, he was determined to take the test.

Run up that ladder...put out that fire...carry that hose across the lot...little Santos marched on and on.

The lieutenant said, "Today you take the final exam." Little Santos began to sweat because he knew his reading was not as good as everyone else. He pleaded to God, "Please help me pass the test."

Little Santos jumped up for joy when the results of the test were announced. The lieutenant exclaimed, "oh boy, by far this is the best!"

Little Santos was hired, and wore his uniform with pride.
He was ready for his first fire and his first fire truck ride.